CHINESE COOKING
VEGETARIAN

TARLA DALAL

S&C

Fourteenth Printing : 2005

ISBN : 81-86469-01-X

Price Rs. 189/-

Published & Distributed by : **Sanjay & Company**
353/A-1, Shah & Nahar Industrial Estate, Dhanraj Mill Compound,
Lower Parel (W), Mumbai - 400 013. INDIA.
Tel. : (91-22) 2496 8068 ● Fax : (91-22) 2496 5876 ● E-mail : sanjay@tarladalal.com

Printed by : **Jupiter Prints**, Mumbai

: Designed by :
Mr. Niranjan Kamatkar

: Photography :
Mr. Rajeev Asgaonkar

OTHER BOOKS BY TARLA DALAL

INDIAN COOKING
Tava Cooking
Rotis & Subzis
Desi Khana
The Complete Gujarati Cook Book
Mithai
Chaat
Achaar aur Parathe
The Rajasthani Cookbook
Swadisht Subzian

WESTERN COOKING
The Complete Italian Cookbook
The Chocolate Cookbook
Eggless Desserts
Mocktails & Snacks
Soups & Salads
Mexican Cooking
Easy Gourmet Cooking
Chinese Cooking
Easy Chinese Cooking
Thai Cooking
Sizzlers & Barbeques

MINI SERIES
A new world of Idlis & Dosas
Cooking under 10 minutes
Pizzas and Pastas
Fun Food for Children
Roz Ka Khana
Microwave - Desi Khana
T.V. Meals
Paneer
Parathas
Chawal
Dals
Sandwiches
Quick Cooking New

TOTAL HEALTH
Low Calorie Healthy Cooking
Pregnancy Cookbook
Baby and Toddler Cookbook
Cooking with 1 Teaspoon of Oil
Home Remedies
Delicious Diabetic Recipes
Fast Foods Made Healthy
Healthy Soups & Salads
Healthy Breakfast
Calcium Rich Recipes
Healthy Heart Cook Book
Forever Young Diet
Healthy Snacks New
Iron Rich Recipes New

GENERAL COOKING
Exciting Vegetarian Cooking
Microwave Cooking
Quick & Easy Cooking
Saatvik Khana
Mixer Cook Book
The Pleasures of Vegetarian Cooking
The Delights of Vegetarian Cooking

The Joys of Vegetarian Cooking
Cooking With Kids
Snacks Under 10 Minutes
Ice-Cream & Frozen Desserts
Desserts Under 10 Minutes
Entertaining
Microwave Snacks & Desserts

CONTENTS

I Soups

II Starters

III Main Dishes

IV Desserts

V Basic Recipes

INTRODUCTION

In recent years, Chinese food has gained increasing popularity in India, particularly in the larger cities. In fact, Chinese cooking is no longer the preserve of the ethnic Chinese and a sizeable number of Indian cooks have now become highly competent if not expert in preparing Chinese dishes —— although naturally, within a limited range. The emphasis in Chinese cooking being on non-vegetarian fare, I have been pressed to bring out a book on Chinese vegetarian food which has resulted in this book.

Like India, China is a vast country with pronounced differences in regional cuisines. I have tasted elaborate vegetarian banquets in Beijing, Tianjin, Shanghai and Guangzhou (Canton) and therefore find it easy to appreciate why the Cantonese style of cooking with its delicious sauces is more attuned to Indian tastes. In contrast, Beijing cuisine for example is bland and its vegetarian fare, being based on soyabean curd cheese (tofu), is not very appealing to the Indian palate. Similarly, soyabean nuggets which are used widely in Chinese Buddhist restaurants as a substitute for meat have yet to gain popularity among Indian vegetarians. The Cantonese and, to some extent, the Schezuan styles of cooking continue to remain the most appealing to Indians and this book is accordingly based on these styles.

Whilst the Chinese use a variety of cooking methods, their unique contribution to the culinary arts is stir frying. A Chinese immigrant to USA described the process as "a big fire – shallow fat – continual stirring – quick frying of cut-up material with wet seasoning". The food to be cooked is first cut in a manner which exposes the maximum surface for cooking (e.g. cut into small pieces, diagonally into thin pieces etc) so that it requires the minimum time to cook. The items are then dropped in a small quantity of hot oil and stirred constantly so that each item receives an even amount of heat. In this

5

way, the process of cooking by stir frying can be completed in a few minutes whilst retaining the nutritional value and the crunchiness of the food.

A final word about flavouring agents. The Chinese had earlier developed whitish savoury powders for taste enhancing which were made mostly from gluten of flour. Around the nineteen hundred and twenties, a Japanese firm manufactured mono sodium glutamate from hydrolysed gluten and sold it under the name Ajinomoto meaning "prime element of taste". And over the years, the use of mono sodium glutamate in Chinese cooking became widespread and at times even excessive in Chinese restaurants resulting in the well-known Chinese restaurant syndrome (first identified in 1968) wherein after enjoying a hearty meal, the diner comes out with a burning sensation in the stomach, headache, numbness and at times even coronary palpitations. There is some controversy about whether mono sodium glutamate is related to this syndrome and some bodies which have conducted blind studies have concluded that the substance is generally safe. The use of this flavouring agent as an additive to infant foods is banned in some countries including India. For adults, however, there does not appear to be any clear evidence against occasional moderate use in home preparations and I have accordingly included it as an optional ingredient.

Tarla Dalal

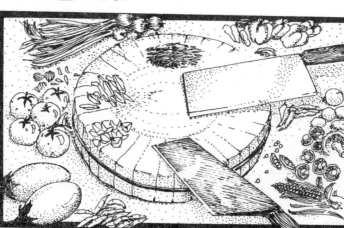

KITCHEN EQUIPMENT FOR CHINESE COOKING

Over the past several centuries, the Chinese have refined their methods of cutting food with the objective of reducing the requirement of cooking oil and fuel to a minimum. The principle they adopt is to cut the food in various interesting ways (eg. diagonally, cubes, strips etc) so that the maximum surface area is exposed for cooking and so that the food pieces are roughly of even size and cook evenly at fast heat. Accordingly, the manner of cutting becomes an important and critical part in Chinese cooking and the method used in many recipes requires that equal attention is paid to both the cutting and the cooking. For cutting purposes, the Chinese use sharp cleavers (usually of 2 to 3 different weights) using the pressure of the whole hand on the top of the handle. The food being cut is placed on a heavy wooden chopping block (about 100 to 150 mm thick) made of solid wood which does not chip off during the cutting process. An expert Chinese cook uses cleavers with great skill and cuts food in different shapes at high speed. Of course, the cutting can be done with any sharp knife but the time required would be correspondingly greater.

The Chinese ingenuity is also seen in their basic cooking vessel – the wok – which is essentially a cone shaped vessel with a rounded bottom. This special shape enables even spreading of heat to all parts and shortens the cooking time. It also ensures that the ingredients return to the centre after stirring. Woks with one handle are used for stir frying so that the food can be easily tossed around from time to time with a view to ensuring even cooking. In contrast, woks with two handles, being more stable, are better suited for placing on a stove and hence are used for cooking by other methods. Traditionally, woks made of iron are used because iron retains the heat better; and such woks are cleaned and then dried over moderate heat regularly after use with a view to preventing rust formation. Although the wok is more suited and effective for Chinese cooking, it can be substituted by other cooking vessels like a skillet or a shallow frying pan for stir frying and by a deeper pan or kadai for deep frying.

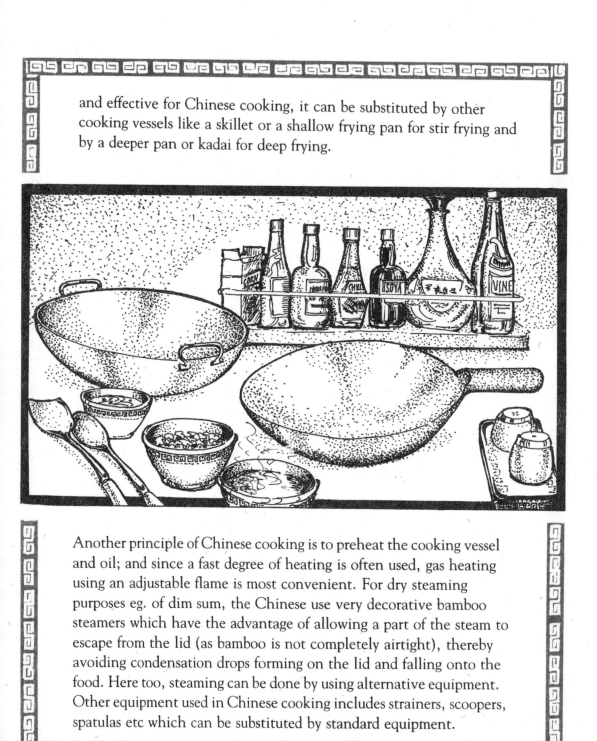

Another principle of Chinese cooking is to preheat the cooking vessel and oil; and since a fast degree of heating is often used, gas heating using an adjustable flame is most convenient. For dry steaming purposes eg. of dim sum, the Chinese use very decorative bamboo steamers which have the advantage of allowing a part of the steam to escape from the lid (as bamboo is not completely airtight), thereby avoiding condensation drops forming on the lid and falling onto the food. Here too, steaming can be done by using alternative equipment. Other equipment used in Chinese cooking includes strainers, scoopers, spatulas etc which can be substituted by standard equipment.

Notes regarding Chinese cooking and ingredients

HOW TO STIR FRY

One of the 4 most important method of cooking Chinese food, it retains the natural colour of the vegetables while keeping them crunchy.

To stir fry, heat the oil in a wok on a high flame. Then add the vegetables in the hot oil and cook for a few minutes while stirring all the time.

You may add the seasoning, particularly Ajinomoto, while frying as it helps faster cooking.

HOW TO DEEP FRY

Cook the food in a deep layer of hot fat.

OIL FOR FRYING OR COOKING

In Chinese cooking, sesame (til) oil is generally used but some people prefer using refined corn oil.

Use as little oil as possible while sautéeing or stir frying since excess oil tends to kill the natural flavour of the vegetables.

VEGETABLES

The vegetables used in Chinese cooking which are easily available in India are:

	Capsicums	
Baby corn (in major cities)	Carrots	Spring onions
Bamboo shoots (in major cities)	Cauliflower	French beans
Moong beans (for bean sprouts)	Celery	Green chillies
Mushrooms (fresh and dry)	Cucumbers	Cabbages

Vegetables which can be eaten raw like capsicums, cabbages, spring onions, fresh mushrooms and cucumbers are generally used in raw form. They are sliced or chopped as required and added directly into a soup or sautéed.

HOW TO PARBOIL VEGETABLES

Baby corn
Carrots
Cauliflower
French beans

1. Put plenty of water to boil.
2. Add the vegetables and cook them for 2 to 3 minutes until crunchy.
3. Do not cover the vegetables while boiling. Use as required.

HOW TO BLANCH SPINACH

1. Put plenty of water to boil. When the water starts boiling, switch off the heat.
2. Put the spinach leaves in the boiling water for a few minutes and then remove them. Be sure not to keep them too long as otherwise, they will lose colour.

HOW TO USE DRY MUSHROOMS

1. Soak dry mushrooms in water for at least 20 to 30 minutes.
2. When thoroughly soaked, they will expand to twice their original size and become soft and spongy. Then chop off and discard the stalks and use only the caps as required.

HOW TO USE CHINESE DRIED BLACK MUSHROOMS

1. Soak the mushrooms in boiling water for 20 minutes.
2. Cut off and discard the stalks. Chop each mushroom cap into half for use as required.

HOW TO PREPARE BEAN SPROUTS

Preparation time : 3 days. No cooking. Makes 3 cups.

1   cup whole moong beans

1. Soak moong beans in water for 24 hours.
2. Drain and rinse until the water is clear.
3. Spread muslin cloth over a vessel, preferably a colander (i.e. one having a few holes at the bottom).
4. Spread the soaked beans over the muslin cloth and cover with another wet muslin cloth. Keep this vessel in a dark place.
5. Sprinkle water over the cloth twice daily for 3 days.
6. On the 4th day, the sprouts will be about 5 cms long.
7. Wash the sprouts and refrigerate until required.

USE OF CORNFLOUR MIXTURE FOR THICKENING

A cornflour mixture in the proportion of 3 level tablespoons of cornflour to 1/2 teacup of water can be used to thicken soups,vegetable gravies etc. Before you start preparing a Chinese meal, prepare such a mixture and keep ready for use as may required. Be sure to stir the mixture well before pouring it as the cornflour tends to settle down. The quantity to be used depends upon the thickness required for the dish.

HOW TO COOK RICE

1. The rice should be small grained and preferably without a flavour of its own. Do not use Basmati or Delhi rice.
2. Cook the rice in plenty of water. When cooked, drain the water. ·
3. Add ½ teaspoon of salt and 1 tablespoon of refined oil while the rice is being cooked. This will help the grain to separate and cook well.
4. After the rice is cooked, remove and spread either on a large tray or on a clean dry cloth so that the grains remain separate.
5. For the preparation of Chinese fried rice, the rice should be cooked well in advance (at least two hours beforehand).

HOW TO COOK NOODLES

1. Put plenty of water to boil. When it starts boiling, add the noodles.
2. Add 1 teaspoon of salt and 1 tablespoon of refined oil while the noodles are being cooked.
3. When the noodles are cooked, they will rise to the top of the vessel and also change colour. The best way to test whether noodles are cooked is to taste them.
4. When the noodles are cooked, remove from the fire and immediately strain in a colander (or large soup strainer) under cold running water. This helps the noodles to separate.
5. If the noodles are to be used after some time, wash them again in cold water to separate them just before use. Alternatively, add 1 tablespoon of refined oil, mix well with a fork and keep aside till required.

Green peas soup

Light and nutritious.

Preparation time :
20 minutes.

Cooking time :
10 minutes.

Serves 6.

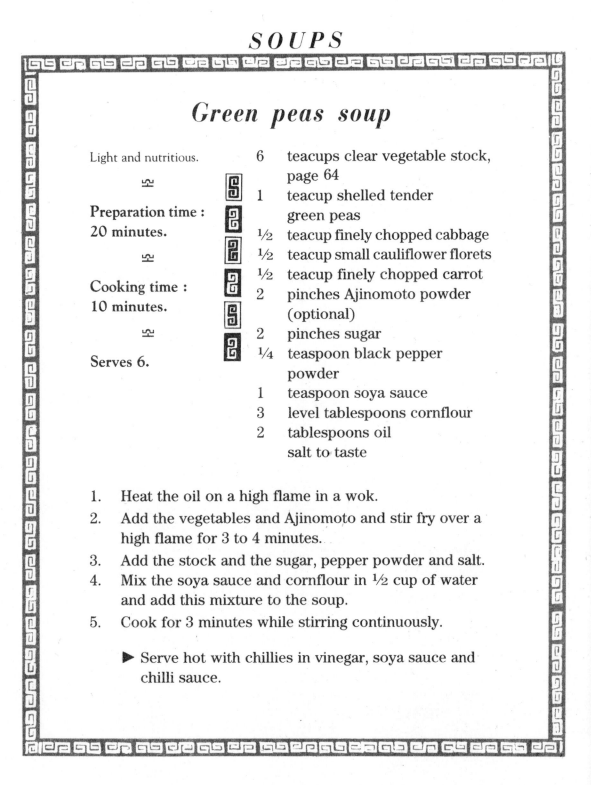

6   teacups clear vegetable stock,
     page 64
1   teacup shelled tender
     green peas
½   teacup finely chopped cabbage
½   teacup small cauliflower florets
½   teacup finely chopped carrot
2   pinches Ajinomoto powder
     (optional)
2   pinches sugar
¼   teaspoon black pepper
     powder
1   teaspoon soya sauce
3   level tablespoons cornflour
2   tablespoons oil
     salt to taste

1.   Heat the oil on a high flame in a wok.
2.   Add the vegetables and Ajinomoto and stir fry over a
     high flame for 3 to 4 minutes.
3.   Add the stock and the sugar, pepper powder and salt.
4.   Mix the soya sauce and cornflour in ½ cup of water
     and add this mixture to the soup.
5.   Cook for 3 minutes while stirring continuously.

▶ Serve hot with chillies in vinegar, soya sauce and
  chilli sauce.

Spinach soup

A light hot soup for spinach lovers.

Preparation time : 5 minutes.

Cooking time : 5 minutes.

Serves 6.

15 to 20 spinach leaves, cut into big pieces
1 clove garlic, crushed
6 teacups clear vegetable stock, page 64
2 tablespoons Chinese dried mushrooms or other canned mushrooms
1 tablespoon soya sauce
1 tablespoon butter
½ tablespoon oil
salt and pepper to taste

For the topping
1 teaspoon sesame oil

1. Remove the stalks from the dried mushrooms and soak the mushrooms in ½ cup of water for 30 minutes.
2. Add the soaked mushrooms without the water to the stock.
3. Heat the butter and oil. Add the garlic and fry for 1 minute.
4. Add the spinach and stir fry over a high flame for 1 minute.
5. Add the stock, soya sauce and boil for 2 minutes.
6. Add salt and pepper.

► Sprinkle sesame oil on top and serve hot with chillies in vinegar, soya sauce and chilli sauce.

Sour and hot soup

Spicy and filling –
for cold days.

ॐ

Preparation time :
20 minutes.

ॐ

Cooking time :
5 minutes.

ॐ

Serves 6.

½ teacup shredded cabbage
½ teacup grated carrot
½ teacup small cauliflower
   florets
½ teacup chopped spring onions
   with greens
1 tablespoon chopped coriander
2 pinches Ajinomoto powder
   (optional)
5 teacups clear vegetable stock,
   page 64
2 tablespoons brown vinegar
1 tablespoon soya sauce
1 teaspoon chilli sauce
½ teaspoon black pepper
   powder
3 tablespoons cornflour
2 tablespoons oil
   salt to taste

For the topping
chopped coriander

1. Heat the oil in a wok on a high flame. Add the
    vegetables and Ajinomoto and stir fry over a high flame
    for 2 minutes.
2. Add the stock, vinegar, soya sauce, chilli sauce, pepper
    powder and salt and cook for 2 minutes.

3. Mix the cornflour in ½ teacup of water and add to the soup. Boil for 1 minute while stirring continuously.

    ▶ Top with coriander and serve hot with chillies in vinegar, soya sauce and chilli sauce.

Chinese vegetable trio soup

A colourful light soup.

Preparation time: 5 minutes.

Cooking time: 5 minutes.

Serves 6.

6   teacups clear vegetable stock, page 64
1   teacup mushrooms, sliced or baby corn (parboiled)
1   teacup carrots, sliced (parboiled)
10 to 12 whole spinach leaves
½   teaspoon oil
    salt to taste

1. Put the stock to boil.
2. Add the mushrooms and carrots and boil for 2 to 3 minutes.
3. Add the spinach leaves and salt. Boil for a few seconds.
4. Trickle the oil on top.

    ▶ Serve hot with chillies in vinegar, chilli sauce and soya sauce.

Top: Mein Chow Soup, page 20; Bottom: Baby Corn Soup, page 19. ➤

Baby corn soup

Picture on page 17

Light and refreshing.

Preparation time :
15 minutes.

Cooking time :
5 minutes.

Serves 6.

12 baby corn
2 spring onions
4 tablespoons green beans
1 carrot, sliced
3 tablespoons canned
    mushrooms, sliced
2 pinches Ajinomoto powder
    (optional)
6 teacups clear vegetable stock,
    page 64
2 tablespoons oil
    salt to taste

1. Slice the baby corn into big pieces.
2. Slice the spring onions with a few leaves.
3. Heat the oil in a wok on a high flame. Add the baby corn, spring onions, green beans, carrot, mushrooms and Ajinomoto and stir fry for 2 to 3 minutes.
4. Add the stock and salt and boil for ½ minute.

▶ Serve hot with chillies in vinegar, soya sauce and chilli sauce.

NOTE : Instead of canned mushrooms, you can also use dried black Chinese mushrooms.

◀ *Clockwise from top: Wontons, page 29; Crispy Fried Vegetables, page 33; Stuffed Mushroom Buns, page 31; Fried Baby Corn in Schezuan Sauce, page 33.*

Mein chow soup

Picture on page 17

Thick, hot and spicy
with the flavour of
mint and coriander.

≅

**Preparation time :
15 minutes.**

≅

**Cooking time :
10 minutes.**

≅

Serves 6.

6   teacups clear vegetable stock,
page 64
2   tablespoons finely chopped
tomato
2   tablespoons finely chopped
capsicum
2   tablespoons finely chopped
cauliflower
2   tablespoons finely chopped
carrot
2   tablespoons finely chopped
cabbage
1   tablespoon finely chopped
fresh mint leaves
1   tablespoon chopped coriander
2   teaspoons chopped garlic
2   teaspoons chopped ginger
3   teaspoons soya sauce
2   tablespoons cornflour
a pinch Ajinomoto powder
(optional)
2   tablespoons oil
½   teaspoon pepper powder
salt to taste

For the topping
chilli oil, page 70
chopped coriander

1. Heat the oil in a wok on a high flame.
2. Add the mint leaves, coriander, garlic, ginger, vegetables and Ajinomoto and stir fry for 2 to 3 minutes over a high flame.
3. Add the stock, soya sauce, salt and pepper powder.
4. Mix the cornflour in 1 teacup of water and add to the soup. Boil for 1 minute. Top with chilli oil and coriander.

▶ Serve hot with chillies in vinegar, chilli sauce and soya sauce.

Stewed cabbage with mixed vegetables

A light and healthy soup.

❀

Preparation time : 10 minutes.

❀

Cooking time : 15 minutes.

❀

Serves 6.

6 teacups clear vegetable stock, page 64
1½ teacups shredded cabbage
½ teacup cooked corn
½ teacup green beans (papadi beans)
a pinch Ajinomoto powder (optional)
salt to taste

For the topping
chopped spring onions

1. Put the stock to boil. Add the cabbage and boil for 10 minutes.

2. Add the corn, green beans, Ajinomoto and salt and cook for 2 minutes.

▶ Top with spring onions and serve hot.

Tum yum soup

The Thai soup with the intriguing flavour of lemon grass.

≌

Preparation time :
15 minutes.

≌

Cooking time :
10 minutes.

≌

Serves 6.

6   teacups clear vegetable stock, page 64.
1   green chilli, cut lengthwise
10 to 15 canned mushrooms, sliced
10 to 12 cauliflower florets (parboiled)
1   tablespoon roughly chopped lemon grass
2   pinches Ajinomoto powder (optional)
1   teaspoon lemon juice
2 to 3 drops oil
   salt to taste

1. Put the stock to boil.

2. Add the green chilli, mushrooms, cauliflower, lemon grass, Ajinomoto and salt and boil for 2 to 3 minutes.

3. Add the lemon juice and top with oil.

▶ Serve hot with chillies in vinegar, soya sauce and chilli sauce.

Sesame Fingers

An hors d'oeuvre with lots of savour and crunch.

ॐ

Preparation time :
20 minutes.

ॐ

Cooking time :
30 minutes.

ॐ

Serves 10 to 12.

1	big loaf sliced bread
4	spring onions, finely chopped
100	grams finely chopped carrots (parboiled)
100	grams finely chopped french beans
1	large capsicum, finely chopped
1	small head celery, finely chopped
½	teaspoon Ajinomoto powder (optional)
2	potatoes
2	teaspoons soya sauce
1	teaspoon chilli powder
1	teacup plain flour
1	tablespoon sesame seeds
4	tablespoons refined oil
	salt to taste
	oil for deep frying

To serve
chilli sauce

1. Boil the potatoes and mash them coarsely.

2. Heat the oil in a wok or frying pan over a high flame. Add the onions, carrots, french beans, capsicum, celery and Ajinomoto and stir fry for 3 to 4 minutes.

3. Add the potatoes, soya sauce, chilli powder and salt and cook for 3 minutes. Cool the mixture.

4. Put a little mixture on each bread slice and press well by hand.

5. Make a paste of the flour in ½ teacup cf water. Apply this paste over the vegetables.

6. Sprinkle the sesame seeds over the vegetables.

7. Deep fry the bread slices in oil.

8. Cut each slice into 4 long strips.

▶ Serve hot dotted with chilli sauce.

Variation: Bean Sprouts Titbits. Instead of vegetables, use bean sprouts and proceed as above.

Corn Rolls

Ideal for cocktail and tea parties.

☙

Preparation time : 10 minutes.

☙

Cooking time : 20 minutes.

☙

Makes 20 rolls.

10 bread slices
2 tablespoons plain flour
  oil for deep frying

For the filling
1 teacup canned sweet corn, cream style
1 onion, chopped
1 green chilli, finely chopped
1 teaspoon soya sauce
¼ teaspoon Ajinomoto powder (optional)
2 tablespoons oil
  salt and pepper to taste

To serve

1   teaspoon chilli sauce

For the filling

1. Heat the oil and fry the onion and green chilli for ½ minute.

2. Add the sweet corn, soya sauce, Ajinomoto, salt and pepper. Mix well and cook till the mixture becomes dry. Cool.

How to proceed

1. Steam the bread for 1 minute and roll out with a rolling pin so that it becomes thinner.

2. On the corner of each slice, spread a little filling and roll into cylinder shape.

3. Make a paste of the flour with 2 tablespoons of water.

4. Seal the edges of the rolls from all sides with a little flour paste.

5. Deep fry in oil until golden brown.

6. Cut each roll into two.

▶ Serve with chilli sauce.

Cauliflower in Schezuan sauce

Crunchy and yummy.

≗

Preparation time : 20 minutes.

≗

Cooking time : 15 minutes.

≗

Serves 6.

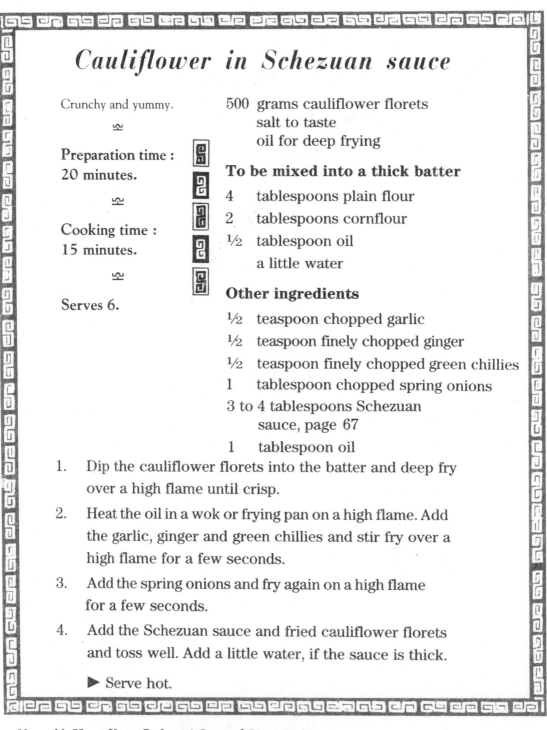

500 grams cauliflower florets
salt to taste
oil for deep frying

To be mixed into a thick batter

4 tablespoons plain flour

2 tablespoons cornflour

½ tablespoon oil

a little water

Other ingredients

½ teaspoon chopped garlic

½ teaspoon finely chopped ginger

½ teaspoon finely chopped green chillies

1 tablespoon chopped spring onions

3 to 4 tablespoons Schezuan sauce, page 67

1 tablespoon oil

1. Dip the cauliflower florets into the batter and deep fry over a high flame until crisp.

2. Heat the oil in a wok or frying pan on a high flame. Add the garlic, ginger and green chillies and stir fry over a high flame for a few seconds.

3. Add the spring onions and fry again on a high flame for a few seconds.

4. Add the Schezuan sauce and fried cauliflower florets and toss well. Add a little water, if the sauce is thick.

▶ Serve hot.

Vegetable Hong Kong Style with Steamed Rice, page 41

➤

Wontons

Picture on page 18

An ever popular
Chinese starter.

≗

**Preparation time :
20 minutes.**

≗

**Cooking time :
25 minutes.**

≗

Serves 4.

For the wontons

wonton wrappers, page 69
oil for deep frying

For the wonton stuffing

1   teacup boiled noodles
2   teacups finely chopped cabbage
2   onions, finely chopped
1   carrot, grated
1   teacup bean sprouts
½   teaspoon Ajinomoto powder
    (optional)
1   teaspoon soya sauce
2   tablespoons oil
    salt to taste

To serve

green garlic sauce, page 71
chilli garlic sauce, page 65

For the tempering

(for steamed wontons)
2   teaspoons chopped garlic
2   tablespoons chopped
    spring onions
½   teaspoon chopped
    green chillies
1   tablespoon oil
    salt to taste

← *Clockwise from top: Hakka Noodles, page 45; Chinese Style Potato Vegetable, page 46;
Stir Fried Beans, Capsicum & Tomatoes, page 51.*

For the wonton stuffing

1. Heat the oil in a wok or frying pan on a high flame. Add the cabbage, onions, carrot, bean sprouts and Ajinomoto and stir fry over a high flame for 3 minutes.

2. Add the noodles, soya sauce and salt.

For the wontons

1. Roll out the wrapper dough into thin circles of about 65 mm. diameter.

2. Put a little stuffing in the centre of each dough circle and fold over to make a semi-circle. Bring the ends together and press.

3. Repeat with the remaining dough and stuffing.

For fried wontons

1. Deep fry the wontons in oil.

2. Serve with green garlic and chilli garlic sauce.

For steamed wontons

1. Arrange the wontons on a greased plate and steam for 10 minutes.

2. Prepare the tempering by heating the oil in a wok or frying pan on a high flame and stir frying the garlic, spring onions and green chillies for a few seconds. Add salt.

3. Pour the tempering over the steamed wontons and serve hot.

Stuffed mushroom buns

Picture on page 18

An ideal snack at any place and time.

≈

**Preparation time :
1 hour.**

≈

**Cooking time :
15 minutes.**

≈

Makes 16 buns.

For the buns

500 grams plain flour

10 grams dry yeast

20 grams fresh yeast

2½ teaspoons sugar

1 teaspoon salt

1 tablespoon butter

For the filling

2 teacups fresh mushrooms, chopped

1 onion, finely chopped

½ teaspoon finely chopped ginger

½ teaspoon finely chopped garlic

½ teaspoon finely chopped green chilli

2 teaspoons cornflour

1 tablespoon tomato sauce

2 tablespoons oil
salt to taste

For the buns

1. Sieve the flour. Make a well in the centre.

2. Add the yeast and sugar. Pour warm water on top and leave for 5 minutes until froth comes on top.

3. Add the salt and butter and make a soft dough by adding some more warm water.

4. Knead the dough very well for 5 to 7 minutes.

5. Cover the dough and leave for at least 1/2 hour or till double in size.

6. When double in size, knead the dough again for 1 minute.

7. Divide the dough into 16 parts, make small balls and put on greaseproof paper. Leave for 20 to 25 minutes or until double in size.

For the filling

1. Heat the oil in a wok or frying pan on a high flame. Add the onion and stir fry over a high flame for a few seconds. Add the ginger, garlic and green chilli and fry again for a few seconds.

2. Add the mushrooms and cook for 2 minutes.

3. Mix the cornflour in 1/4 cup of water and add to the mixture.

4. Add the tomato sauce and salt and cook for 1 to 2 minutes.

How to proceed

1. Stuff each dough round with a little mushroom filling.

2. Put the rounds on a greaseproof paper and leave for 20 to 25 minutes or until double in size.

3. Steam for at least 15 minutes.

   ▶ Serve hot.

Crispy fried vegetables

Picture on page 18

A popular
Chinese starter.

≅

Preparation time :
10 minutes.

≅

Cooking time :
15 minutes.

≅

Makes 25 pieces.

3 teacups vegetables
(baby corn, capsicums, cabbage
and cauliflower), cut into long
strips
oil for deep frying

For the batter

5 tablespoons cornflour

5 tablespoons plain flour

1/2 teaspoon ginger-garlic paste

1/4 teaspoon black pepper powder

1/4 teaspoon Ajinomoto powder
(optional)

1 teaspoon lemon juice

To serve

green garlic sauce, page 71
and Schezuan sauce, page 67

1. Mix the ingredients for the batter and add enough water
to make a thick batter.

2. Dip the strips into the batter and deep fry in oil.

▶ Serve hot with green garlic sauce and Schezuan sauce.

Onion pancakes

A popular starter
for the meal.

Preparation time :
10 minutes.

Cooking time :
20 minutes.

Makes 20 to 25
small pieces.

For the pancakes

½   teacup cornflour
½   teacup plain flour
½   teacup milk
½   teacup water
     a pinch salt
2   teaspoons melted butter or oil

For the filling

3   teacups chopped spring
     onions with leaves
1   tablespoon réfined oil
½   teaspoon Ajinomoto powder(optional)
     a pinch sugar
     salt to taste

Other ingredients

oil for deep frying

For the pancakes

1.   Mix all the ingredients into a batter.

2.   Spread 1 tablespoon of the batter onto a non-stick
     frying pan and cook on both sides with a little oil.
     Repeat for the remaining batter.

For the filling

1.   Heat the oil in a wok or frying pan on a high flame,
     add the onions and Ajinomoto and cook for 2 minutes.

2. Add the sugar and salt and remove from the heat.

3. Drain the liquid, if any.

How to proceed

1. Spread 1 tablespoon of the filling on each pancake, fold and if desired, seal the edges by applying a little of the pancake mixture.

2. Deep fry in oil.

▶ Cut into pieces and serve hot.

Variation: Coconut Pancakes. Proceed in the same manner using a filling of a mixture of 1 teacup of grated fresh coconut, ½ teacup of sugar and 1 drop of rose or vanilla essence (optional) instead of the above filling. And after filling this mixture into the pancakes, sprinkle sesame seeds on top before frying.

Sweet and sour ginger

A tasty accompaniment to your meal.

ℒ

Preparation time : 5 minutes.

ℒ

No cooking.

ℒ

Makes 1 cup.

3 tablespoons finely chopped or sliced tender ginger

For the herbal sauce
1 tablespoon powdered sugar
2 teaspoons white vinegar
½ teacup water
 juice of 1 lemon
2 pinches salt

For the herbal sauce

1. Mix the sugar, vinegar, water, lemon juice and salt.
2. If required, adjust the sweetness by adding more powdered sugar.

How to proceed

Mix the ginger with the sauce.

▶ Serve as an accompaniment.

Spring rolls

Preparation time :
30 minutes.

Cooking time :
30 minutes.

Serves 10.

For the stuffing

2	teacups mixed vegetables (french beans, carrots, cabbage)
100	grams boiled noodles
1	teacup bean sprouts
2	onions, sliced
2	teaspoons soya sauce
¾	teaspoon Ajinomoto powder (optional)
4	tablespoons refined oil
	salt to taste

Clockwise from top: Chinese Vegetables in Hot Garlic Sauce, page 48; Corn and Bean Sprouts, page 44; Chinese Steamed Bread, page 53.

For the pancakes

½ teacup cornflour
½ teacup plain flour
½ teacup milk
½ teacup water
  a pinch salt
2 teaspoons melted butter or oil

Other ingredients
oil for deep frying

For the stuffing

1. Cut the vegetables into long thin strips.
2. Heat the oil in a wok or frying pan on a high flame. Add the onions, vegetables, bean sprouts and Ajinomoto and stir fry on a high flame for 3 to 4 minutes.
3. Add the noodles, soya sauce and salt and cook for 2 minutes. Cool and keep aside.

For the pancakes

1. Mix all the ingredients into a batter.
2. Spread 1 tablespoon of the batter onto a non-stick frying pan and cook on both sides with a little oil. Repeat for the remaining batter.

How to proceed

1. Spread 1 tablespoon of the filling on each pancake, fold and if desired, seal the edges by applying a little of the pancake mixture.
2. Deep fry in oil.

   ▶ Cut into pieces and serve hot.

Top: Pan Fried Noodles, page 57; Bottom: Broccoli & Baby Corn Vegetable, page 52.

Steamed rice topped with creamy vegetables

Picture on front cover

Delicately flavoured rice and vegetables.

≗

Preparation time :
15 minutes.

≗

Cooking time :
10 minutes.

≗

Serves 4.

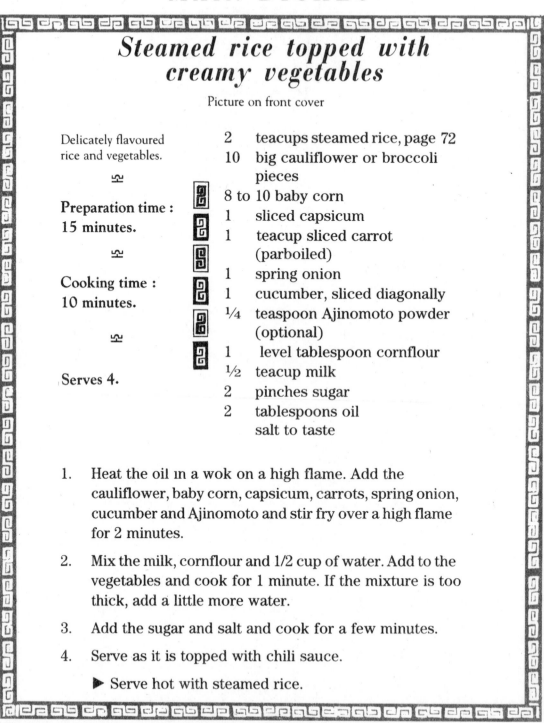

2	teacups steamed rice, page 72
10	big cauliflower or broccoli pieces
8 to 10	baby corn
1	sliced capsicum
1	teacup sliced carrot (parboiled)
1	spring onion
1	cucumber, sliced diagonally
¼	teaspoon Ajinomoto powder (optional)
1	level tablespoon cornflour
½	teacup milk
2	pinches sugar
2	tablespoons oil
	salt to taste

1. Heat the oil in a wok on a high flame. Add the cauliflower, baby corn, capsicum, carrots, spring onion, cucumber and Ajinomoto and stir fry over a high flame for 2 minutes.

2. Mix the milk, cornflour and 1/2 cup of water. Add to the vegetables and cook for 1 minute. If the mixture is too thick, add a little more water.

3. Add the sugar and salt and cook for a few minutes.

4. Serve as it is topped with chili sauce.

    ▶ Serve hot with steamed rice.

Vegetable Hong Kong style
with steamed rice

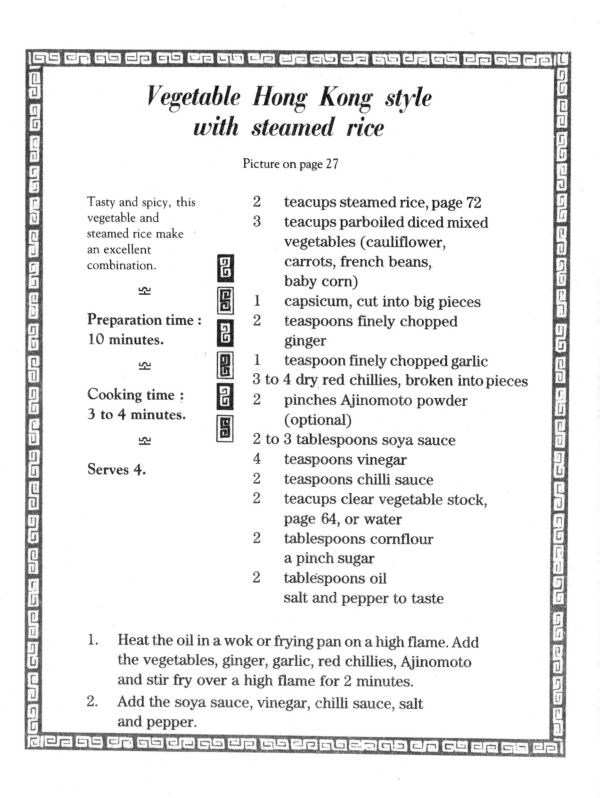

Picture on page 27

Tasty and spicy, this
vegetable and
steamed rice make
an excellent
combination.

~

Preparation time :
10 minutes.

~

Cooking time :
3 to 4 minutes.

~

Serves 4.

2   teacups steamed rice, page 72
3   teacups parboiled diced mixed
    vegetables (cauliflower,
    carrots, french beans,
    baby corn)
1   capsicum, cut into big pieces
2   teaspoons finely chopped
    ginger
1   teaspoon finely chopped garlic
3 to 4 dry red chillies, broken into pieces
2   pinches Ajinomoto powder
    (optional)
2 to 3 tablespoons soya sauce
4   teaspoons vinegar
2   teaspoons chilli sauce
2   teacups clear vegetable stock,
    page 64, or water
2   tablespoons cornflour
    a pinch sugar
2   tablespoons oil
    salt and pepper to taste

1.   Heat the oil in a wok or frying pan on a high flame. Add
     the vegetables, ginger, garlic, red chillies, Ajinomoto
     and stir fry over a high flame for 2 minutes.

2.   Add the soya sauce, vinegar, chilli sauce, salt
     and pepper.

3.   Mix the stock and cornflour, add to the mixture and cook for 1 minute. Add the sugar.

▶ Top with the steamed rice and serve hot.

Vegetable Manchurian

Picture on page 55

The ever-popular Chinese dish.

⌇

Preparation time : 15 minutes.

⌇

Cooking time : 20 minutes.

⌇

Serves 4.

For the Manchurian

4   teacups cabbage, finely chopped
1-½ teacups carrots, grated
1   onion, chopped
2   tablespoons cornflour
5   tablespoons plain flour
3 to 4 cloves garlic, finely chopped
1   green chilli, finely chopped
2   pinches black pepper
¼   teaspoon Ajinomoto powder (optional)
       salt to taste
       oil for deep frying

For the sauce

1   tablespoon garlic, finely chopped
2   teaspoons green chillies, finely chopped
2   teaspoons ginger, finely chopped

1	tablespoon cornflour
1	teacup clear vegetable stock, page 64 or water
1	tablespoon soya sauce
2	pinches sugar
2	tablespoons oil salt to taste

For the Manchurian

1. Mix the cabbage, carrots, onion, cornflour, plain flour, garlic, green chilli, Ajinomoto, salt and pepper.
2. Shape spoonfuls of the mixture into small balls. If you find it difficult to form balls, sprinkle a little water.
3. Deep fry in hot oil until golden brown.

For the sauce

1. Heat the oil in a wok or frying pan on a high flame. Add the garlic, green chillies and ginger and stir fry over a high flame for a few seconds.
2. Mix the cornflour with ¼ cup of water.
3. Add the stock, soya sauce, cornflour mixture, sugar and salt and cook for a few minutes.

How to serve

Just before serving, put the balls in the sauce and cook for a few minutes.

▶ Serve hot.

Corn and bean sprouts

Picture on page 37

For the corn lovers.

Preparation time :
10 minutes.

Cooking time :
5 minutes.

Serves 4.

2 teacups cooked corn
2 teacups bean sprouts
1 teaspoon chilli - garlic paste, page 70
½ teacup tomato purée
1 tablespoon tomato ketchup
1 tablespoon cornflour
2 tablespoons oil
salt to taste

1. Heat the oil in a wok or frying pan on a high flame. Add the chilli - garlic paste and stir fry over a high flame for a few seconds.
2. Add the tomato purée and tomato ketchup and stir fry for 1 minute.
3. Add the corn, bean sprouts and salt and cook again for 1 minute.
4. Mix the cornflour in ½ cup of water and add to the vegetables. Cook again for 1 minute.

▶ Serve hot.

Hakka noodles

Picture on page 28

Vegetables and noodles make a meal by itself.

≅

Preparation time :
10 minutes.

≅

Cooking time :
5 minutes.

≅

Serves 6.

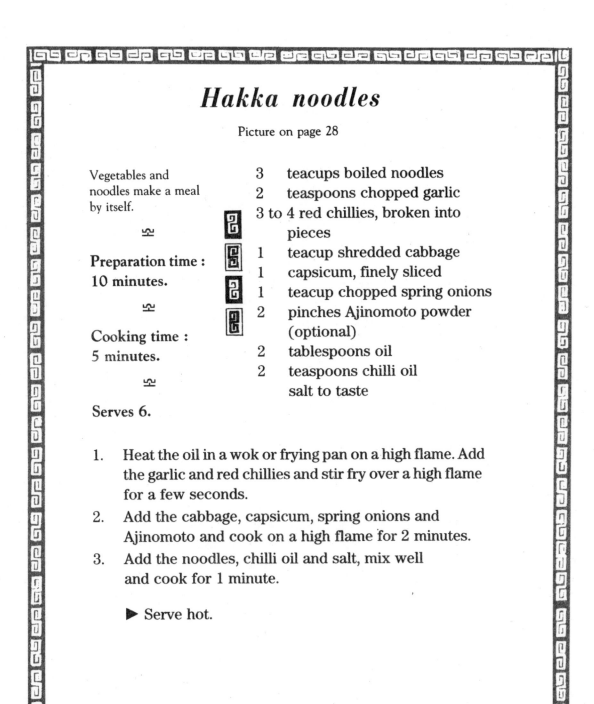

3   teacups boiled noodles
2   teaspoons chopped **garlic**
3 to 4 red chillies, broken into pieces
1   teacup shredded cabbage
1   capsicum, finely sliced
1   teacup chopped spring onions
2   pinches Ajinomoto powder (optional)
2   tablespoons oil
2   teaspoons chilli oil
    salt to taste

1.   Heat the oil in a wok or frying pan on a high flame. Add the garlic and red chillies and stir fry over a high flame for a few seconds.

2.   Add the cabbage, capsicum, spring onions and Ajinomoto and cook on a high flame for 2 minutes.

3.   Add the noodles, chilli oil and salt, mix well and cook for 1 minute.

▶ Serve hot.

Chinese style potato vegetable

Picture on page 28

Serve as a main dish as well as a starter.

જી

Preparation time :
10 minutes.

જી

Cooking time :
10 minutes.

જી

Serves 4.

4   large potatoes (80% cooked)
1   teaspoon chopped garlic
½   teaspoon chopped ginger
1   teaspoon chopped
       green chillies
1   teaspoon tomato ketchup
2   tablespoons soya sauce
½   teaspoon chilli sauce
2   teaspoons cornflour
4   tablespoons oil
      salt to taste

For the garnish
sliced spring onions

1.   Cut the cooked potatoes into fingers.

2.   Heat the oil in a wok or frying pan on a high flame. Add the potato fingers and cook on a high flame for a few minutes. Remove from the wok or frying pan and keep aside.

3.   In the same oil, add the garlic, ginger and green chillies and stir fry for a few seconds. Add the potato fingers, tomato ketchup, soya sauce, chilli sauce and salt.

4. Mix the cornflour in ½ teacup of water. Add to the mixture and cook for 1 to 2 minutes.

▶ Serve hot topped with sliced spring onions.

Three treasure vegetables

Colourful, simple and tasty.

Preparation time : 15 minutes.

Cooking time : 5 minutes.

Serves 4.

1   teacup asparagus (from can)

1   teacup baby corn (parboiled)

1   teacup soaked and sliced black mushrooms or button mushrooms (from can)

1   level tablespoon cornflour

1   teacup milk

2   pinches sugar
    salt to taste

1. Arrange the asparagus, baby corn and mushrooms in a serving dish.

2. Mix the milk and cornflour with ½ cup of water and cook for 1 minute. Add the sugar and salt.

3. Spread this mixture on top of the vegetables.

▶ Serve hot.

Chinese vegetables in hot garlic sauce

Picture on page 37

A spicy version of sweet and sour vegetables.

ೱ

**Preparation time :
10 minutes.**

ೱ

**Cooking time :
10 minutes.**

ೱ

Serves 4.

10	big cauliflower pieces
1	capsicum, sliced
10	baby corn (parboiled)
10	french beans (parboiled), sliced
	a pinch Ajinomoto powder (optional)
2	teaspoons finely chopped ginger
2	teaspoons finely chopped garlic
2	teaspoons finely chopped green chillies
½	teacup tomato purée
2	teaspoons cornflour
2	tablespoons oil
	salt to taste

1. Heat the oil in a wok or frying pan on a high flame. Add the ginger, garlic and green chillies and stir fry over a high flame for a few seconds.

2. Add the vegetables and Ajinomoto and cook for a few minutes.

3. Add the tomato purée.

4. Mix the cornflour in ½ teacup of water and add to the vegetables.

5. Add salt and cook for a few minutes. If you like, add a pinch of sugar.

▶ Serve hot.

Vegetable munshu

Picture on page 55

These delicious tortillas stuffed with stir fried vegetables make a complete meal.

෴

Preparation time :
20 minutes.

෴

Cooking time :
20 minutes.

෴

Serves 6.

For the tortillas

2   teacups plain flour

2   teaspoons oil

2   pinches salt

For the stir fried vegetables

½   teacup sliced carrots

½   teacup shredded cabbage

½   teacup shredded capsicum

½   teacup bean sprouts

2   pinches Ajinomoto powder (optional)
    a pinch sugar

2   tablespoons oil
    salt to taste

For the plum sauce

12   plums

5   tablespoons sugar

1   teaspoon chilli powder

2   pinches salt

For the tortillas

1.   Mix all the ingredients. Make a soft dough by adding enough water.

2.   Knead the dough well and keep aside for 30 minutes.

3. Roll out small thin rounds of 150 mm. diameter and cook them on both sides on a tava (griddle).

For the stir fried vegetables

1. Heat the oil in a wok or frying pan on a high flame.

2. Add the remaining ingredients and stir fry for 2 minutes.

For the plum sauce

1. Slice the plums.

2. Add the sugar, chilli powder and salt and cook on a slow flame until soft.

3. Blend into a smooth sauce in a liquidiser.

4. Adjust the sweetness according to taste.

How to serve

Spread some plum sauce on each tortilla, place some vegetables in the centre, roll up and serve.

Stir fried beans, capsicum and tomatoes

Picture on page 28

Quick and nourishing.

卐

Preparation time :
15 minutes.

卐

Cooking time :
5 minutes.

卐

Serves 4.

1 teacup bean sprouts
1 teacup sliced tomatoes (without seeds)
1 teacup sliced capsicum
a pinch Ajinomoto powder (optional)
soya sauce (optional)
1 tablespoon oil
salt to taste

1. Heat the oil in a wok or frying pan on a high flame. Add the bean sprouts, tomatoes and capsicum and stir fry over a high flame for a few seconds.
2. Add the Ajinomoto and salt and cook for 2 minutes.
3. If you like, sprinkle a little soya sauce on top.

▶ Serve hot.

Broccoli and baby corn vegetable

Picture on page 38

Cashewnuts provide crunch as well as taste to this dish.

ॐ

Preparation time :
10 minutes.

ॐ

Cooking time :
5 minutes.

ॐ

Serves 4.

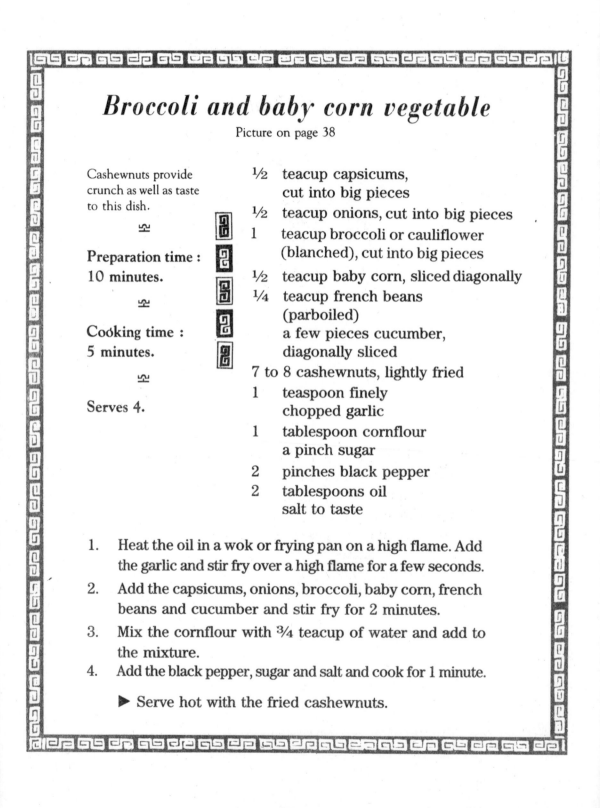

½ teacup capsicums, cut into big pieces

½ teacup onions, cut into big pieces

1 teacup broccoli or cauliflower (blanched), cut into big pieces

½ teacup baby corn, sliced diagonally

¼ teacup french beans (parboiled)
a few pieces cucumber, diagonally sliced

7 to 8 cashewnuts, lightly fried

1 teaspoon finely chopped garlic

1 tablespoon cornflour
a pinch sugar

2 pinches black pepper

2 tablespoons oil
salt to taste

1. Heat the oil in a wok or frying pan on a high flame. Add the garlic and stir fry over a high flame for a few seconds.

2. Add the capsicums, onions, broccoli, baby corn, french beans and cucumber and stir fry for 2 minutes.

3. Mix the cornflour with ¾ teacup of water and add to the mixture.

4. Add the black pepper, sugar and salt and cook for 1 minute.

▶ Serve hot with the fried cashewnuts.

Chinese steamed bread

Picture on page 37

Easy to make,
this bread tastes
slightly sweet.

Preparation time :
1 hour.

Cooking time :
15 minutes.

Makes 16 pieces.

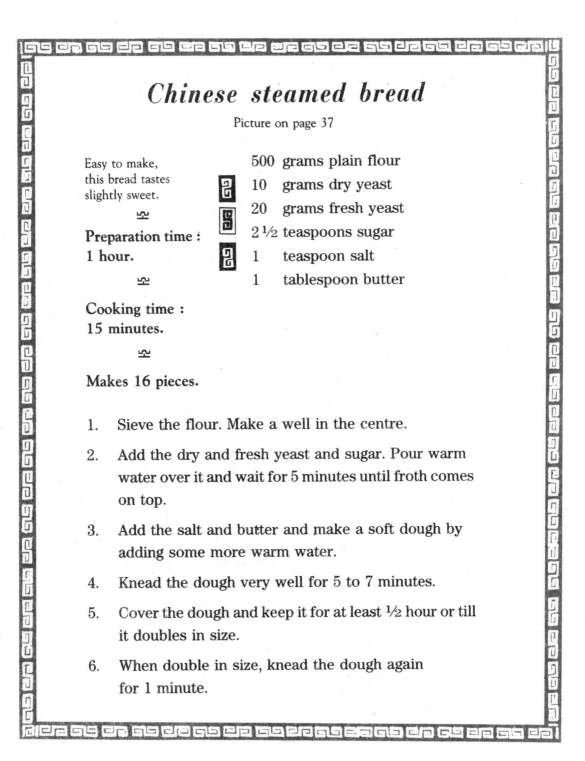

500 grams plain flour
10 grams dry yeast
20 grams fresh yeast
2 ½ teaspoons sugar
1 teaspoon salt
1 tablespoon butter

1. Sieve the flour. Make a well in the centre.

2. Add the dry and fresh yeast and sugar. Pour warm water over it and wait for 5 minutes until froth comes on top.

3. Add the salt and butter and make a soft dough by adding some more warm water.

4. Knead the dough very well for 5 to 7 minutes.

5. Cover the dough and keep it for at least ½ hour or till it doubles in size.

6. When double in size, knead the dough again for 1 minute.

7. Divide the dough into 16 parts, make small balls and put them on greaseproof paper.

8. Leave the rounds aside for 20 to 25 minutes or till they are double in size.

9. Steam the rounds for at least 15 minutes.

▶ Serve warm.

French beans and garlic

A quick Chinese vegetable.

Preparation time : 10 minutes.

Cooking time : 5 minutes.

Serves 4.

6 teacups french beans, cut diagonally
3 cloves garlic, crushed
1 teaspoon sugar
3 teaspoons soya sauce
3 tablespoons oil
salt to taste

1. Blanch the french beans in boiling salted water for a few minutes. Drain and plunge into cold water.

2. Heat the oil in a wok or frying pan. Add the crushed garlic. Before it turns brown, add the french beans and stir fry for 1 minute.

3. Add the sugar, soya sauce and salt. Continue stirring for another minute.

▶ Serve hot.

Clockwise from top: Stir Fried Vegetables for Munshu; Vegetable Munshu, page 49; Vegetable Manchurian, page 42. ➤

Pan Fried Noodles

Picture on page 38

A meal by itself.

Preparation time :
10 minutes

Cooking time :
5 minutes.

Serves 4.

3 teacups boiled noodles
3 tablespoons oil

For the vegetables

1 can mushrooms (400 grams)
1½ teacups green peas
1 tablespoon finely chopped garlic
1 tablespoon finely chopped green chillies
3 to 4 tablespoons soya sauce
1 heaped tablespoon cornflour
¾ teacup water
a pinch Ajinomoto (optional)
2 tablespoons oil

For the vegetables

1. Heat the oil in a wok on a high flame and add the garlic, green chillies and fry for a few seconds.

2. Add the mushrooms and peas and cook for a while.

3. Mix the soya sauce, cornflour and water. Add to the vegetable. Add a little salt and Ajinomoto if you like.

For the noodles

1. Heat the oil in a frying pan,

2. Spread the noodles over it and cook on a low flame until the noodles are brown at the bottom. Flip over and cook until the noodles are brown again.

How to proceed

Spread the noodles in a plate and top with the vegetables.

▶ Serve hot.

Anticlockwise from top: Date and Sesame Wontons, page 58 and Coconut Pancakes, page 61; Goreng Pisang, page 63; Honeyed Noodles with Vanilla Ice-Cream, page 59.

Date and sesame wontons

Picture on page 56

A healthy dessert for
the date lovers.

⌣

Preparation time :
30 minutes.

⌣

Cooking time :
20 minutes.

⌣

Makes 20
wontons.

For the wontons

20   wonton wrappers, page 69
½   teacup milk
2   tablespoons powdered sugar
   oil for deep frying

For the stuffing

¼   teacup sesame seeds
½   teacup brown sugar
½   teacup chopped dates
1   tablespoon soft butter

To serve

vanilla ice-cream

For the stuffing

1. Toast the sesame seeds on a medium flame until they are golden. Cool.
2. Crush them coarsely.
3. Mix with the brown sugar, dates and butter.

How to proceed

1. Place about 1 teaspoon of the stuffing in the centre of each wonton wrapper.
2. Pull the edges of the dough around the filling and with the help of a little milk, twist to seal like a money bag.
3. Deep fry in oil until golden. Cool.
4. Sprinkle the powdered sugar on top.

▶ Serve hot with vanilla ice-cream.

NOTE: You can also top with warm honey and serve hot.

Honeyed noodles with vanilla ice-cream

Picture on page 56

Even the kids will love the noodles.

❧

Preparation time : 15 minutes.

❧

Cooking time : 1 minute.

❧

Serves 4.

4 teacups crispy noodles, page 69

4 roasted almonds, cut into pieces

For the honey sauce

1 tablespoon sugar

1 tablespoon honey

To serve

vanilla ice-cream

1. In a small vessel, heat the sugar and 1 teaspoon of water on a slow flame.

2. When the sugar melts, immediately add the honey, mix well and pour over the noodles. Sprinkle the almond pieces on the top.

▶ Serve with vanila ice-cream.

Toffee apples

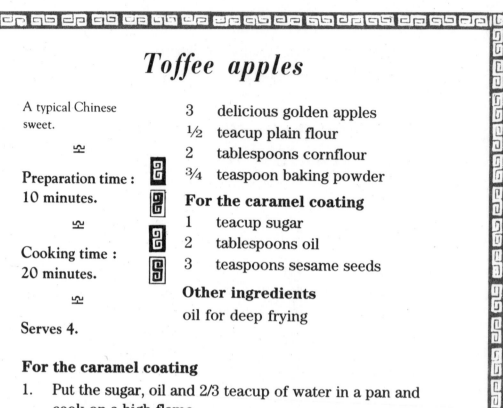

A typical Chinese sweet.

స

Preparation time : 10 minutes.

స

Cooking time : 20 minutes.

స

Serves 4.

3   delicious golden apples
½   teacup plain flour
2   tablespoons cornflour
¾   teaspoon baking powder

For the caramel coating

1   teacup sugar
2   tablespoons oil
3   teaspoons sesame seeds

Other ingredients

oil for deep frying

For the caramel coating

1. Put the sugar, oil and 2/3 teacup of water in a pan and cook on a high flame.

2. When the mixture begins to bubble, shake the pan continuously to prevent burning.

3. Continue cooking and shaking the pan until the syrup is light brown in colour.

4. Remove from the heat, add the sesame seeds and mix well.

How to proceed

1. Mix the plain flour, cornflour and baking powder in a bowl. Add water and stir into a smooth, thick batter.

2. Peel, core and cut the apples into bite-size pieces.

3. Coat the apple pieces evenly with the batter and deep fry in hot oil until golden.

4. Fill a serving bowl with ice-cubes and cover with water.

5. Put the fried apples in the caramel syrup and coat evenly. Drain well and plunge into the ice-cubes bowl. Keep for a few minutes till the caramel coating hardens. Drain thoroughly.

▶ Serve.

Variation : Toffee Bananas. Proceed as above substituting apples by bananas pieces.

Coconut pancakes

Picture on page 56

You will love the fresh rich coconut filling.

Preparation time : 5 minutes.

Cooking time : 10 minutes.

Makes 12 pancakes.

For the pancakes

½ teacup cornflour
½ teacup plain flour
½ teacup milk
½ teacup water
1 tablespoon sesame seeds
2 teaspoons melted butter or oil
a pinch salt
oil for frying

To be mixed into a filling

1 teacup grated fresh coconut
½ teacup sugar
1 drop rose or vanilla essence (optional)

To serve

vanilla ice-cream

For the pancakes

1. Mix the cornflour, plain flour, milk, water, butter and salt into a batter.

2. Spread 1 big spoon of the batter onto a non-stick frying pan of about 190 mm. diameter and shake the pan in a circular motion so as to spread the batter evenly. Cook firstly on one side until done and then on the other side.

3. Repeat with the remaining batter.

How to serve

1. Spread 1 tablespoon of the filling on each pancake and fold. If desired, seal the edges by applying a little of the pancake mixture.

2. Sprinkle some sesame seeds on top and fry until crisp.

▶ Serve with vanilla ice-cream.

Goreng pisang (Fried bananas)

Picture on page 56

This is practically a national snack among the migrant populations in South East Asia who serve it with scoops of coconut or mango ice-cream. An exotic way to treat bananas.

~

Preparation time : 10 minutes.

~

Cooking time : 10 minutes.

~

Serves 4.

4 bananas, peeled and cut into halves
oil for deep frying

For the batter

4 tablespoons self-raising flour
4 tablespoons rice flour
1 tablespoon cornflour
2 pinches salt

For sprinkling

2 tablespoons brown sugar

To serve

coconut or mango ice-cream

1. Mix the self-raising flour, rice flour, cornflour, ½ cup of water and salt into a smooth paste.
2. Dip the banana halves in the batter and deep fry in oil until golden in colour.
3. Roll in the brown sugar.

▶ Serve with ice-cream.

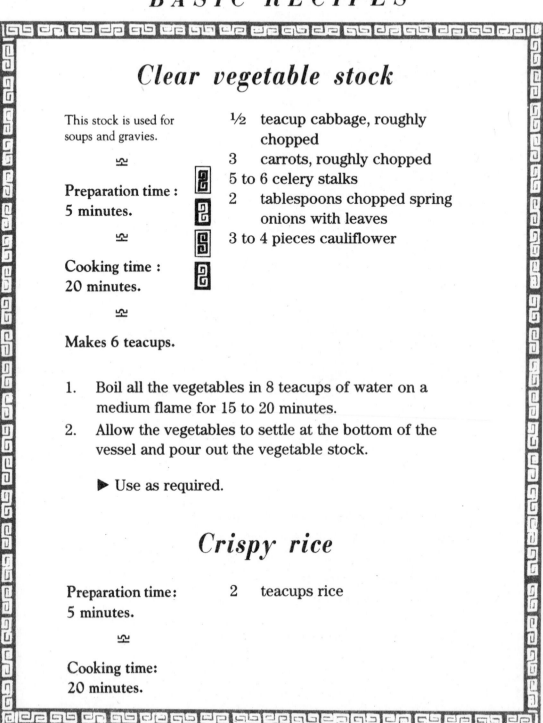

Clear vegetable stock

This stock is used for
soups and gravies.

☙

Preparation time :
5 minutes.

☙

Cooking time :
20 minutes.

☙

Makes 6 teacups.

½   teacup cabbage, roughly
     chopped
3   carrots, roughly chopped
5 to 6 celery stalks
2   tablespoons chopped spring
     onions with leaves
3 to 4 pieces cauliflower

1. Boil all the vegetables in 8 teacups of water on a
    medium flame for 15 to 20 minutes.
2. Allow the vegetables to settle at the bottom of the
    vessel and pour out the vegetable stock.

    ▶ Use as required.

Crispy rice

Preparation time:
5 minutes.

☙

Cooking time:
20 minutes.

2   teacups rice

1. Put plenty of water to boil. Add the rice and cook.
2. When the rice is 95% cooked, drain out the water.
3. Spread the rice on a large tray, cover with a piece of cloth and sun dry until crisp.

▶ Store in an air-tight bottle and use as required.

NOTE: This rice lasts for 3 to 4 months.

Chilli garlic sauce
(Shung tung sauce)

Can be served with an appetizer.

≈

Preparation time : 10 minutes.

≈

No cooking.

≈

Makes 1 cup.

1	teacup finely minced tomatoes
1	tablespoon grated garlic
½	tablespoon grated ginger
½	teaspoon chopped green chillies
1	tablespoon chopped coriander
1	tablespoon tomato ketchup
1	teaspoon white vinegar
¼	teaspoon powdered sugar
1	teaspoon chilli oil, page 70
	a pinch Ajinomoto powder (optional)
	salt to taste

Mix all the ingredients in a liquidiser for a few seconds and blend into a smooth sauce.

▶ Use as required.

Fried noodles

Preparation time :
5 minutes.

卐

Cooking time :
20 minutes.

卐

Serves 4.

200 grams Chinese fine noodles
oil for frying
salt to taste

1.   Put plenty of water to boil and add 2 tablespoons of oil.
     Add the noodles while stirring occasionally and cook
     until tender. Drain well.
2.   Spread the noodles on a clean piece of cloth and allow
     to dry for at least 2 to 3 hours.
3.   Heat the oil in a wok or frying pan over medium heat.
     Fry small quantities of noodles at a time in the hot oil
     until golden brown.
4.   Remove the noodles from the oil and drain throughly.
     Repeat with the remaining noodles.

Schezuan sauce (for cooking)

Preparation time :
10 minutes.

Cooking time :
5 minutes.

Makes 1½ cups.

For the paste

20 red chillies
5   cloves garlic

Other ingredients

1   tablespoon finely chopped garlic
1   teaspoon finely chopped green chillies
½   tablespoon grated ginger
2   tablespoons finely chopped onions
1   teaspoon finely chopped celery
1   tablespoon cooking vinegar
¾   teacup clear vegetable stock, page 64
1   tablespoon cornflour mixed with 2 tablespoons of water
1½ teaspoons white vinegar
2   teaspoons sugar
    a pinch Ajinomoto powder (optional)
3   tablespoons oil
    salt to taste

For the paste
1. Put plenty of water to boil.
2. Add the red chillies and garlic and cook for 8 to 10 minutes. Cool.

3. Drain out the water. Grind into a smooth paste in a liquidiser using a little water.

How to proceed

1. Heat the oil in a wok or frying pan and fry the garlic, green chillies, ginger, onions and celery for 1 minute.
2. Add the paste and fry again for 1 minute.
3. Add the cooking vinegar and cook for 1 minute. Add the stock and mix well.
4. Add the cornflour mixture, white vinegar, sugar, Ajinomoto and salt. Cook for 1 minute while stirring throughout.

▶ Use as required.

Red garlic sauce

Serve as a table sauce.

〜

Preparation time : 5 minutes.

〜

Cooking time : a few minutes.

〜

Makes 1 ½ cups.

1 tablespoon finely chopped garlic

½ teaspoon finely chopped green chillies

1 tablespoon finely chopped spring onions

1 tablespoon finely chopped onion

1 tablespoon tomato ketchup

1 teacup clear vegetable stock, page 64

1 tablespoon cornflour mixed with 2 tablespoons of water

a pinch Ajinomoto powder (optional)

2 tablespoons oil
salt to taste

1. Heat the oil in a wok or frying pan on a high flame and fry the garlic, green chillies, spring onions and onion for 1 minute.
2. Add the tomato ketchup, clear vegetable stock and cornflour mixture. Mix well and cook for 1 minute.
3. Add the Ajinomoto and salt.

▶ Use as required.

Wrapper dough for wontons and crispy noodles

Preparation time :
15 minutes.

2   teacups plain flour
½   teaspoon salt

છ

Cooking time :
10 minutes.

1. Sieve the flour and salt together.
2. Add hot water gradually and make a soft dough.
3. Knead for a while and keep for 30 minutes.
4. Apply oil on your palm and knead the dough until it becomes bouncy and elastic.
5. Roll out thinly into desired shapes. For wonton wrappers, roll into small circles. For crispy noodles, roll out into a 200 mm. diameter circle, cut into strips and deep fry in oil until crisp.

Chilli garlic paste

Preparation time :
30 minutes.

Cooking time :
1 minute.

10   cloves garlic
5 to 7 red dry chillies

1. Soak the chillies in a little water for 30 minutes. Then boil for 1 minute.
2. Grind with the garlic in a mixer.

   ▶ Use as required.

Chilli oil

Preparation time :
2 hours.

Cooking time :
a few seconds.

Makes 1 cup.

15 to 20 red chillies
1   teacup oil

1. Break the red chillies into big pieces.
2. Heat the oil on a high flame and add the chillies. Immediately switch off the gas.

3. Cover and allow to stand for 2 hours. Strain and store in a bottle.

▶ Use as required.

Chillies in vinegar

Preparation time :
a few minutes.

၉

No cooking.

၉

Makes 1 cup.

6 to 7 green chillies
1   teacup white vinegar

Cut the green chillies and add to the white vinegar.

▶ Use as required.

Green garlic sauce

Preparation time :
5 minutes.

၉

No cooking.

၉

Makes ½ cup.

1   tablespoon finely chopped coriander
1   tablespoon chopped green chillies
1   tablespoon chopped garlic or 2 tablespoons finely chopped fresh garlic
     juice of 1 lemon
1   tablespoon powdered sugar

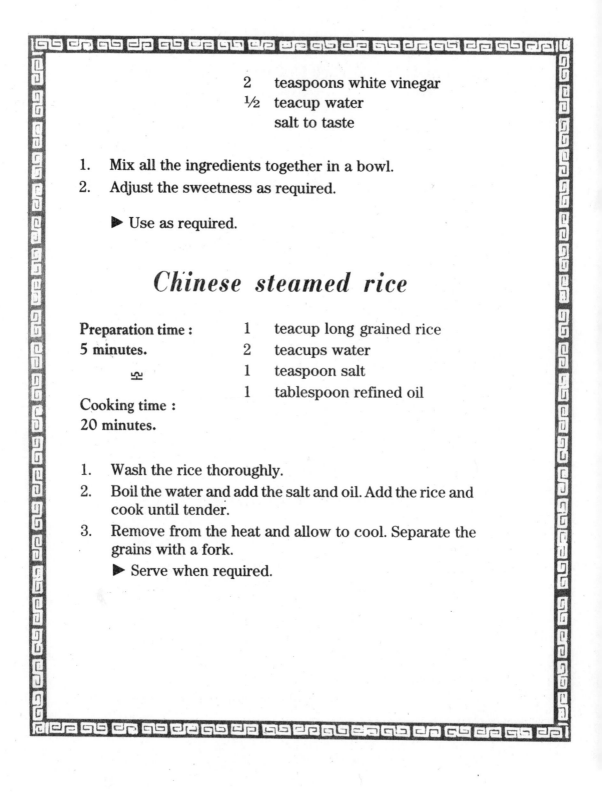

2   teaspoons white vinegar
½   teacup water
    salt to taste

1.   Mix all the ingredients together in a bowl.
2.   Adjust the sweetness as required.

▶ Use as required.

Chinese steamed rice

Preparation time :
5 minutes.

🕉

Cooking time :
20 minutes.

1   teacup long grained rice
2   teacups water
1   teaspoon salt
1   tablespoon refined oil

1.   Wash the rice thoroughly.
2.   Boil the water and add the salt and oil. Add the rice and cook until tender.
3.   Remove from the heat and allow to cool. Separate the grains with a fork.

▶ Serve when required.